Pra...
Su...

'A rich mix of character study and personal narrative, which masterfully walks the line between imagination and truth.'

—Dean Atta

'Here is a fresh, strikingly original, distinctive first collection. The strong, gutsy poems – each a well-crafted entity in itself – demonstrate a striking young talent worth noting. In her already assured voice, with teasing overtones at times of Sylvia Plath, Anne Sexton and Carol Ann Duffy, Elizabeth Ridout demonstrates her wide range. The heady mix of surreal touches versus the almost brutally real, updated classical and literary allusions, and the arresting lexis leave the reader 'breathless' with awe.'

—Patricia McCarthy

'Elizabeth Ridout's debut collection is a dazzling mix of daring and accomplishment. The confessional elements in her work are presented to her readers with a restraining craft that gives the candour of approach and rawness of subject matter memorable utterance. Ridout works from a range of settings and voices, and incorporates a raft of influences (from Patti Smith to Anne Sexton and the Beats), but she makes these distinctively her own. We enter Ridout's world to "feast on the sudden awakenings/ and spiralling moments", as she has it, in poems that fizz off the page.'

—Peter Carpenter

Summon

Elizabeth Ridout

SUMMON

First published in 2020 by
Myriad Editions
www.myriadeditions.com

Myriad Editions
An imprint of New Internationalist Publications
The Old Music Hall, 106–108 Cowley Rd,
Oxford OX4 1JE

First printing
1 3 5 7 9 10 8 6 4 2

A CIP catalogue record for this book
is available from the British Library

ISBN (pbk): 978-1-912408-42-9
ISBN (ebk): 978-1-912408-43-6

Designed by WatchWord Editorial Services, London
Typeset in Dante by www.twenty-sixletters.com

Printed and bound in Great Britain
by CPI Group (UK) Ltd, Croydon CR0 4YY

'But it's no use now,' thought poor Alice, 'to pretend to be two people! Why, there's hardly enough of me left to make one respectable person!'

—*Lewis Carroll*, Alice in Wonderland

Contents

A Photograph of My Mother, 18,
    in August 1977   1

Insomnia Chamber   3

Nine Pints   5

Ana   7

Bluebird   9

Ariadne   11

One Night   13

The Taxidermist   15

Summon   17

Fairlight Beach   19

Husband   20

Fortune Teller   21

Dinner Table   24

The Magician's Assistant   25

Runaways in the Woods   26

The Little Buddha   28

A Man and His Goat, in Moscow   30

Hoarder   31

Inked   33

Jim Morrison on 101   36

The Pear Tree and the Caravan   40

Abortion   42

Wall   43

A Photograph of My Mother, 18, in August 1977

You began me with a cry to a god
who wasn't listening.
I flew in like those forty-year-old
dandelion clocks at your feet
to a Madonna in platforms and suede.

My fingertips sing out for yours.
I saw you through a rose quartz, at first—
now you are a yellowing snapshot

standing at the end of a garden path.
Mouth mimicking the endless O of the lens,
in a permanently airborne kiss
that flutters across decades.

Eyes squeezed joyfully
against the flare of flash and flame of roses—
you know nothing
and are revelling in it.

Were you waiting for me?

Holding your hands up
to ward off the camera's approving nod
like a mask it is a pleasure to wear,
fingertip faced.
I am a glint in the camera's eye

before I grabbed you round the middle
and you belonged to me.

Insomnia Chamber

These are the records
of the Insomnia Chamber.
It's always four thirty-seven in the morning
here, so let's crack on.

Last night, we brought up the current
drought of sleeping,
which left you dry-mouthed, gasping
for the blessedness,
the cool cave of a closed lid;
we negotiated with yesterday's nightmare
about a circus girl who was afraid of clowns
and what that might mean
about your relationship with your father.

My future clerk,
in some cases, it is inevitable that you will go
completely mad sorting through dreams.
Slightly green around the edges,
the recurring ones
tend to be a little bitter, like an angry olive,
or a piece of Christmas coal.

Those from childhood often have a creamy
phlegm over them, like custard
or banana yoghurt.

This needs to be removed,
if they are to be dealt with.

The vivid ones need time to solidify
from simple passion and colour,
until you can crack them open like lychees
and feast on the sudden awakenings
and spiralling moments inside.

Nine Pints

I'll have nine pints, please,
stick a straw in your ear,
slurp you down like a milkshake.
I'll take the whole thing
unvarnished, unwaxed.
Don't panic, baby,
I just see your body
as transport for that head,
unlike others.
Plastic nails,
dirty geisha knees—Kali in tight trousers
with rictus lipstick and kitten tongue, clutching
the coiffed scalps of willing victims,
butter-pat hair and movie-villain eyebrows,
Marilyn-breathless—fuzzy, never angry,
a meringue shimmying
in perfect Rorschach symmetry
through the shards
of men's devotions
and women's bitterness.

That's you.

I could eat you for every breakfast,
like a supplement or a giant pill
for what ails—you would improve me,
work on my insides, a tonic
to take in, take you on,
amalgamate us and
put you on, new uniform.

But, as I cannot flay away your appeal,
and you have navigated your way out
of the spoiled bedding
of the various misfortunes I visited upon you,
you must be the victim of lightning strikes,
wild animal stampedes, exploding Tube carriages,
anything that could be condensed
into Nabokovian parentheses, and stomped out
like a heart.

That's how this will work.

Ana

I am what it is to become nothing,
becoming important through erasure—
I am eating you from the inside out.

One, two, three, four
countable sources of Eve
lying flat; I scream victory
through the proud jut
of arrowhead hipbones.

Insomniac baby,
curled up in an ironic position.

There's nothing to me.
There's nothing to you,
with your decay-scented
mouth-juices and knobbly
spine.

Arachnid-kneed
controller of flies—
wanton girl—
I am a glossy eyed disappearing act

that will leave you breathless;
a weightless stoning,
a gaping cement overcoat.

Bluebird

I fucked a man who killed a bluebird.
He told me all about it
over crystal stems and bleeding rump,
by the light of a tasteless moon
and oozing candle stump,
how he had hit it with his slick black car
on his way to meet me here.

I had no time to clean it up, he smiled,
tongue running over his teeth,
like the phlegm of a mollusc around a shell,
and laughing,

explained to me
how he had driven himself
here with the thing caged
in the grille—
a twitching mess.

He poured himself another drink
and flickered underneath the chandelier.
He had a soft belly
and careful hair and tasted beige.

We ripped each other open, an act.

In the morning, I left
before I had to talk to him again,
backing out of the hall
like a barefoot burglar in a dog's garden.

The drive was still,
clouds crinkled on the edge of the eye watching.
Trees were shaking,
and I couldn't hear birdsong.

Ariadne

Everyone's always agreed I've got great legs.
So, I suppose, it's not unreasonable to give me
a few more (even if they are a bit hairier). But
seriously, that girl has always had it in for me.

Insecure, you know—
some people can't cope with competition.
It's natural talent, I can't fight that.
Other women always have been jealous of me
and my pretty eyes (all six of them).

If she won't handle a bit of healthy rivalry
then that's her problem. So petty!

I'm a creative person
(I'm well known for it), I've just diversified—
getting into decorating nooks, crannies,
those bits behind the bathroom sink.
Now, I'm infamous
(especially among the insect community).

It goes to show,
pride doesn't have to come before a fall.

I always bungee-snap back
on my unbreakable spirit
and satin suspender strings.

One Night

Damply fizzing with lust,
like two plastic beakers of Cava,
we have been crashing into
and obliterating each other's empty spaces.
Baptismal night air
corrupted with cigarette smoke—
the awkwardness of the exodus,
contra dancing up the stairs,
staring each other out.

There is nothing in this room
but stained nylon sheets
and the smell of transience.
You push into blackness,
but the door is left open
and the hall light left on.
You are saying things to me
I wouldn't like my mother to hear.

The aftermath—
minutes of slimy embarrassment
and disengagement,
and a half-lionhearted offer to brave outside

where my rancid pumpkin awaits
at the street corner.
Each of us reduced to
a human snapshot taken by the other,
to be fished out at will for a quick
pick-me-up.

The Taxidermist

Shaved-leg prickle,
palely veined as a pebble,
taupe as a split sausage—your paw-pink rawness
pickled, like an eyeball
for a blindfolded Halloween game.

An indecency of stitching could frame you—
needle you into place,
like a saddle for a penny farthing,
padding for a fainting couch,
or stuffing for a brothel bench.

Lie still, this will hurt—
he can mount you
in mahogany or rosewood.
He can put you in a bell jar for a literary flourish
and to keep away the fleas,

dress you up
in a voodoo jazz cat's shrunken-head top hat
or the bonnet of a mouse
on the Havisham cake, perhaps
the apron of a rat from the Lovetts' kitchen.

He has Growltiger's eyepatch
and Algernon's flowers.
The profane and the sacred
will allow you to be eaten
by these moths instead of those worms.

Summon

Lunchtimers with cotton neck-chains,
arms raised like shamans
invoking the grey end, the collapse of the tunnel,
the putty ceiling to be blasted to the skies.

They meditate on an STD testing poster
for the hundredth time this week.

She gets on at Goodge Street,
painted, chicken-boned, rooster-feathered,
skulls spiralling through her DNA,
a roe doe's head where her womb should be.

Her eyes red as the Central Line.
She is crying, and everyone looks
up, down, through the glass
at their black artery, anywhere else.

She screams, she rolls her head,
a letting of saltwater and bile.
She rings her bells and slams her sticks,
she shakes the snake from her,

she throws herself on brogues and trainers,
ringlets her hips, and licks
the chewing gum off the floor.

A woman in a green coat looks up
at Camden Town—she stands, adjusts her bag,
moves towards the woman
and the gap. She reaches out,

shy as the fox cubs on Holloway Road.
They brush each other's fingertips,
turn to get off in one motion,
as the train sets off with the doors wide open.

Fairlight Beach

The sky is a circus tent—
red, yellow, golden tassels of cloud.
I grab your hand, a prayer.
We waltz in slow motion across the sand,
chopping dusty lines from the horizon.
A swayer, a waggler, and a dangler,
I am a butcher's shop window,
until we fizz in the spray like bath bombs—
dog crap and rat-tails of seaweed
smear across slick rock pates,
judgemental shaking monk's heads in the breeze.
The weep of Nick Drake
warps through a portable radio.
In liquid, our sameness is striking
and comforting—
eyes cut over each other's pieces,
the puckers, the clefts, brains in our jars.
Drunk on whisky and the situation,
I slip on disloyal pebbles
and cut my arm gloriously open.
Only truly naked then, I feel peeled like an egg.
It is kissed better, but I get dressed.

Husband

I see you
as less a prince in shining armour
than a violation in fancy dress.
Precise in everything but compassion, your love
was airless, a mouth—
you were someone to whom people happened.

I have the personality of an electric fence
(I already said farewell to several of me).
We went for each other's faces—
how was I ever so blush, so raw?

I see myself, lissom, lissom,
a child in oversized satin shoes.
I have been so badly behaved that
I think I have learnt everything—
I am a car crash, or bad television.

I can't stop watching us now, a flickering tape
as we perform an emotional peep show
through the cracked surveillance camera
that is my mind's eye.

Fortune Teller

On the cusp of two civilisations,
Nike and Adidas gleam off the cobbles
of the Ottoman Empire.
Neon strip lighting in a fight to the death
with veiled dancers and the wail of a qanun.
A Turkish pop song, underwater sound,
Hamsa-handedly giving us food for memory,
as honey and apple tea float down a back alley.

Metal through her face
and cluttering up her fingers,
she summons freshly-dug
grave-mud for our mouths.
The boy misunderstands
and drinks the whole thing down to the grounds,
flushed out with a wide-eyed glass of water,
accidentally toasting our destiny—
down the hatch.
My cup has a crack down the middle
and feels appropriate.

Landmasses span the edges of this
tiny china world—
patchouli purple, the scrubby velvet
of a second-hand dress leaking black
fringe over the tablecloth.
Fingertips, filthy and elegant,
like used ballet slippers,
fan the cards—they are thick, a prop from a play,
they are definitely objects.

Aslan, Aslan!
This means Daddy, unsurprising.
We are on our way
to our own Cair Paravel, apparently.
We will go to New York for Jess,
(Who is Jess? Oh, jazz!
We shall go to New York for *jazz*)—
two Cinderellas, smelling of cheap cigarettes
and rakı, down to their last lira bill.
I must wear more yellow.
('That's your complexion.')
I write: *she sees*
('You can see that just looking at you.')
We are each other's second great love.
('Not an unusual situation, is it?')

She sees a line down my middle,
makes a shining slashing movement,
and I hear you,
seas and languages and lives away,
talking over my future—
louder than a harras of horseshoes, unavoidable
as a doppelgänger.

Dinner Table

You always had relentlessly white china.
We soldier on in polite determination
chewing through tough subjects
and an equally tough steak and kidney pie.
We are having a wrist-slashingly good time—
names hover between us, conjuring
argument and the ideals of cut-price gurus.
By addressing these divides, we are embroidering
in red along the branches of the family tapestry,
deadheading bloodlines that were dripping
down the generations and on to your tablecloth.

The Magician's Assistant

Jack-o'-lantern empty mouth
scraped clean,
waiting to be filled,
smile lipsticked on to my sawdust head,
soaking everything in.
You push the lever into the small of my back
like a kitchen knife,
throw me around like a voice
into a red leather box.
Lid shuts,
a slit down the centre
for the sword.

You arrived inside a witch's house in the sky,
it landed on top of me,

and I have no feet to poke out.

Runaways in the Woods

It was the winter we spent without
clean underwear
that made me realise it was going to be a disaster.
Frozen cat turds
curled up like soft-scoop by the van—
solid toothbrushes, the inside of the windows
swelling into junkie-veins.
I'd spend hours collecting branches for the fire,
quietly, as carefully as Fagin's children
taking handkerchiefs
from the pockets of the homed.

In this muddy patch, children get sick with
old-fashioned illnesses, diseases with the ring of
'whalebone' or 'crinoline'.
Trees our security guards,
the mole-voice of doubt
chewed on me over and over again,
like an insane baby.

In the evenings, I'd go to bed
in a cardigan and a hat.
You'd wear gloves to play the piano;

I'd wear gloves to write.
It sounded good
to hear about, not to live.

One morning, I woke up
and rats had eaten my records—
my cardboard heroes and models—
and that was the end of that.

The Little Buddha

with thanks to Sabrina Goacher

He was found in a deer-brown industrial bin
round the back of a now-closed Safeway.
He came to them through a maternal bin raid,
Siddhartha's curls chipped, noseless.

Gold slithering from his robes
like a quilt sliding from a bed.
He sat by the electric fire in the front room;
she would sit beneath him, looking.

There had never been softness, silence,
before he arrived.

A gaudy vortex—shorthand for enlightenment—
a wheel on the laminate,
steering in the right direction.

She could gaze for hours at this handy guide—
she would touch his plaster ūrnā,
leave flowers of lined paper at his missing feet.
Until next door brought their boy.

He was found in the garden,
smeared with fox shit and unpoetic moss,
far from the tree, with black rings
around his eyes, wax sealing his mouth—
a red gag. From a child's squat crayon,
an obscenity of a moustache.

She now has an empty space.

A Man and His Goat, in Moscow

I'd forgotten him
in the dark, in the Arbat.
He, to me, was gabbling
in the language of the revolutionary
and the depressive—
we spoke in tongues to each other.
He cradled the kid towards me,
its eyes were foaming, its mouth was open,
and I had a vision of the sky
over Fabergé onions
becoming orange as Veles' oxen heart.
Okudzhava melts, cracks in two.
A squat Yakut—Chort, Chernobog, throat slit.

Astray, guided.

Hoarder

The newspapers are judging her,
she has missed dates.
The birthdays and deaths you don't know
or care about are sepia, a diary of damp

curling across events and crucial moments.
Four tubs of denture cream (she has no teeth left),
a crystal ball from the woo-woo shop
(she never saw anything in it),

a children's party of biscuit cutters,
grubby ribbon, buttons gathered
like a serial killer's trophies in a jar,

Noddy toys she's holding for her friend Big Ears,
royal wedding mugs—
in her house longer than each marriage—
five boxes of china children

she fostered from the tip,
baskets of material with orange plants and
brown flowers (there are no brown flowers),

and bin-bags creased as laugh lines
applaud her with their cocktail-dress rustlings
as she moves through the rooms.

She was a seamstress, once.
She made wedding dresses, baby clothes,
markers of time and lives.

It took her hours,
stitching *cunt* into the seams
of each in tiny letters.
No one ever complained.

She has prophetic dreams
of falling towers of crap, burning mattresses
and dancing silverfish,
glittering as belly dancers.

Wrappers and packets and tissues
holding nothing.
She has cultivated her blank stare, her army.

Inked

Zoom down, a pigeon-shit view
of the needling street lights
poking through the metal shutter
of a kebab shop

with poly blinds above
bandaging the windows of a sad act,
asleep again on the sofa—
faux leather, reminiscent of low quality
S and M.

Under the tingling buzz of a strip light,
un-showered, dinner's flotsam still
in his beard. His arms and legs and neck
are scattered over the ripped seats.

Self-inflicted doodles tumour
across his wrecked epidermis,
scribbled on to the canvas
his mother once bathed.

His arms, particularly, look like the walls
of an abandoned car park.

The snake, rudely scaled and slim of eye,
curls drunkenly across the sinews
of the upper arm, a permanent wriggle
towards the raw slab of neck.

Livid in colour and expression,
the Y of his tongue licks forever
up to the vulnerable ball of the shoulder.

Across from him lies the dragon,
a Chinese-restaurant-menu beast,
violently blue, goggle eyes
green as a beetle's backside.

With every hair that stands on end,
his dustbin-fire breath moves
up towards translucent eyelids.

With every goosebump
the pin-up girl, one eye forever closed,
wiggles.

More Bettie Sentence than Bettie Page,
tasselled like a flesh cushion
and attached, quite literally, at the hip

to a man who could never get a girl like that
another way.
She could strangle you with those breasts,
and you'd like it.

She looks down on to the mermaid,
bursting from a turquoise splash
of a knee breaking on to the upper thigh.

Mouse-nose nipples pointing forever
at an unimpressive scrag of gristle.
Woven into the mesh of this cartoon-stripped
fool's version of eternity.

They will only dissolve when he does.
They are angry, and begin to climb.

Jim Morrison on 101

The car was rented just outside Sunnyvale
from the sort of place you would find
at the end of the world.
Blasted highway, faded ice-cream-cone pumps,
visible filaments, the works.
In the event of a nuclear apocalypse
the only survivors would be cockroaches,
mutants, and here.

Buying into it, a witness to vintage California
from the Yorkshire Dales, the closing of a circle—
the exorcism of the sun-dried bee-hived
Valley Girl mother through this pilgrimage
to her manically dry landscape
from England's depressive soil.

The car. The closest thing to a Cadillac
as budget would allow. Vinyl-covered seats
as slippery as a groupie's tongue,
and twice as fragrant.
Scarred dashboard and oft-slapped radio,
a fractal stream of West Coast sound. No flaws,
apart from the charming.

Lizard-brown spiked spots on the skyline,
with deck shoes on the pedal
and chino shorts pristine despite the dirt.
No breeze, no sound except the screeching
of a now-shattered Stratocaster
from tortoiseshell. Hot tarmac and roadkill.

A sneaky bottle
of Southern Comfort in the glove compartment,
as close to satisfied as it is possible for me to be.
The road screaming into the distance,

and there he is.

Twitching like a skink
python-footed, subtle as cow hide.
I slow down, and he seems to speed up,
coming up fast.
Puts his thumb down by those hips—
cracks a smile. There's the dimple.
I am going his way, Los Angeles, it turns out.
He has no bags; he is vague, poetic.
He squirms like a toad into the passenger seat,
leather on vinyl.

I restart the engine,
the car croons into movement,
and we drive.

He is reassuringly as expected.
He lights a cigarette, we swig SoCo.
We hear a keyboard, and I babble,
'I thought you might be on this route.
I have come from the grey and the grass—
what can I do to please you?
What can I do to make you happy?'

He looks, shepherd curls,
snarls, 'Don't run me a bath when we get there.'
'Wherever we're going.'
'To the other side, brother. Always.'
He pulls a lighter out of his pocket,
calming flare—
and grins at me.
'You were coming my way, remember.'

The cacti swirl. Smoke, the heat. My eyes swim
with pattern, clouds turn to paisley—
his remain fixed on me.

Everything is going south in this shimmering
handbasket of glass and steel.

I was expecting this when I touched
down in Oakland, and now he is beside me,
I have nothing to ask him.

He throws his head back,
that camera-shutter whip of cheekbone and lip,
and laughs
and laughs again.

'Brother, you got nothing to ask me,
you're chasing the red shadow
when you need to find the sun.
At the end, my friend,
all you gotta ask yourself is
is you is, or is you ain't?'

I can no longer see.
The toad's skin is underneath my fingers
and the man next to me
flicks his forked tongue in my ear.

The Pear Tree and the Caravan

for Marcus

We are, technically, homeless.
I don't feel so,
though a well-placed call could
capsize this whole thing.

Rot box—
in the middle of horsey nowhere,
like a severed head hidden in a beautiful park.
A brave little incense stick fights the good fight
alongside the grubby Indian throws, and quilts
with satisfyingly round cigarette burns, that I have
strewn to 'cheer things up',
like painting an old woman's nails—
pointless, but touching.

We are still too poor to go to the dentist,
although you have rescued me—a refugee
from a room above a Chinese takeaway,
at the dubious end of the Holloway Road,
with twenty-three waving cats in the window
that still prowl and greet me at five a.m.

Single-glaze Perspex is covered in a moist sheen,
a body bag of plastic keeping us, like taxidermy
mice, not too warm and not too cold.

Now, it is the hottest summer on record, again,
and I rip the window open
so the pear tree growing on the other side
can drip in, the hand of a grandmother.

In the mornings,
she serves me breakfast, while
you lie next to me on our dirty mattress,
naked and asleep. The fruit falls into my hand,
softly, cleanly, plumply—I bite into it—
happiness trickles down my face.

Abortion

I am an absence
I have the sacred geometry
of a crumpled plastic bag
I am a bursting
a tentacled segment
I am an explosion of nothing
I am the back of your eyelids
I am two faces meeting
I am a crowd
I am making you dizzy
I have a mouth
now I don't
I am an angel with the wings of a moth

A thrown-away poem
an angry scribble on a disliked picture

Wall

for my parents

I was a baby when the wall came down.
I always felt such a rare harmony with it
when watching its ugly smear
at a distance of reels.

Bipolar bear of Berlin,
waking up in the morning one side or the other.
Pale, tired East /
agitated, swashbuckling West—
as hard to pin down as a gingerbread man—
it's a swine when you're in the middle.

I come of age in a time of walls.
It fits, terrible as a spectrum.
Balaclavas donned and placards thrown
by the sleeping bag in the doorway.
We are all cracking like scabs.

I am legion; the Cocteau siblings,
feckless Janus and Martha and George
all throw glasses in my frontal lobe,

Ornias at my right thumb—
all hovering, lying in wait, dormant,
crouching in the brain, in jelly, in fluid,
to squirt from spongy nerves
and confused glands, pouring
through my frame of references.

I would have been so happy
to be the spider or the umbrella case,
to sing in my sleep,
to ward away kishis or Edward Mordrake,
depending on continent.

Maybe, then, there would have been peace.

Original sources

'Ana', 'Ariadne', 'A Photograph of My Mother, 18, in August 1977' and 'The Taxidermist' were all first published in *Agenda, the Ekphrastic issue, Volume 52 No. 3–4*, on 3rd June 2019.

'Ana' also won the Commendation award in the 2017 Creative Future Literary Award, and was published in the prize winners' anthology, *Important Nothings*.

'One Night' first appeared on *Poetry Pulse* online, in January 2017, and subsequently on *Agenda Poetry* online, in *Notes for Broadsheet Poets 31*, accompanying *Volume 52 No. 3–4*, on 3rd June 2019.

Acknowledgements

This collection would not have been possible without inspiration and support from many people.

I would like to thank Matt Freidson at Creative Future, Candida Lacey at Myriad Editions and Victoria Heath Silk for their heart-lifting appreciation, wonderful input and practical support in getting this collection to the light; Dean Atta for his earliest reading, fantastic advice as I began the journey on this new experience, and kind endorsement of the collection; and Patricia McCarthy for her constant encouragement, championship and wonderful words about my work.

All my thanks to Peter Carpenter for all his life-changing patronage and kindness. Thanks also to Jane Commane for her hugely inspiring reading at Ty Newydd.

I will always be grateful to Susie Beckham and Laura Alabaster for constant emotional support; to Emily Derbyshire, Jade Fishbourne, Zoe Holm, Alison Douglas and Tim Ross; to James H. for being my much-loved ally and for introducing me to Patti Smith (all your fault). All my friends—you're all diamond dogs and a glittering, tattooed source of inspiration to me.

I would like to try the impossible task of thanking my parents for all their love, patience, willingness to listen, open-mindedness and infinite kindness—and for forming me from books, art, music and debate. I wouldn't be here without you, in any sense. Love you.

And finally, I would like to thank Marcus Chapman for saving me. You are my constant inspiration every single day and you set me free. Thank you for being the love of my life and my artistic and emotional life raft. Thank you for taking all of me.

About the author

Elizabeth Ridout has published her poetry and reviews in *Agenda*, where she was recently Broadsheet Poet, and in various other publications online. She studied English Literature at Oxford University, and she won a Creative Future Literary Award in 2017. She lives in Tunbridge Wells.

About Spotlight

Spotlight Books is a collaboration between Myriad Editions, Creative Future and New Writing South to discover, guide and support writers whose voices are under-represented.

Our aim is to spotlight new talent that otherwise would not be recognised, and to help writers who face barriers, or lack opportunities, to develop their creative and professional skills in order to create a lasting legacy of work.

Each of our three organisations is dedicated to specific aspects of writer development. Together we are able to offer a clear ladder of support, from mentorship through to development editing and promotional opportunities.

Spotlight books are not only treasures in themselves but also beacons to other under-represented writers. For further information, please visit: www.creativefuture.org.uk

Spotlight is supported by Arts Council England.

'These works are both nourishing and inspiring, and a gift to any reader.'—Kerry Hudson

Spotlight stories

Georgina Aboud
Cora Vincent

Tara Gould
The Haunting of Strawberry Water

Ana Tewson-Božić
Crumbs

Spotlight poetry

Jacqueline Haskell
Stroking Cerberus: Poems from the Afterlife

Elizabeth Ridout
Summon

Sarah Windebank
Memories of a Swedish Grandmother